The Beautiful Leaves

Karen Greenbaum-Maya

LOS ANGELES † NEW YORK † LONDON † MELBOURNE

The Beautiful Leaves by Karen Greenbaum-Maya

978-1-947240-87-2   Paperback

978-1-947240-88-9   eBook

First Printing 2023

Cover photo "Glimpse" by Karen Greenbaum-Maya

Layout and design by Mark Givens

For information:

Bamboo Dart Press

chapbooks@bamboodartpress.com

Bamboo Dart Press 041

www.pelekinesis.com

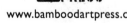
www.bamboodartpress.com

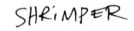
www.shrimperrecords.com

Walter Maya

1929-2018

CONTENTS

THE BEAUTIFUL STORY

Don't say this is a beautiful story.

Don't say he died in his prime.
Don't say he could have had another good twenty years.
Don't say he was marked by the curse of an ancient sin
    coming home. There was no curse,
    there was no sin.
Don't say Western medicine let him down.
Don't say there was still some way for him to live.
Don't say I failed to give everything I had.

Don't say his doctors didn't take him seriously.
Don't say anyone blocked him getting all he needed.
Don't say he took hospice too soon, fooled them all
    and thrived for another decade.
Don't say his death was tragic or comic or absurd.
Don't say he was full of life and laughter to the end.
Don't say he died a good death.

Tell how he wanted to go out to breakfast at 2 a.m.
    and was enraged that he couldn't.
Tell how he realized, furious and defeated,
    he would never again get out of that bed.
Tell how he hated my leaving the room so much,
    he cursed the flowing Schubert piano sonata
    I put on to bridge my absence.

Tell how he begged me to help him go home,
  though we were home.
Tell how he left a voicemail accusing me of leaving him
  alone in an airport parking garage.
Tell how I keep that voicemail,
  my only way left to hear his voice.

FIRST RESPONDERS

1. We Learn to Ask for Lift-and-Assist

I tell 911 *Look for the jacarandas.*
to find our house, at the basin end of the cul-de-sac,
flanked by the lemon tree, the plum,
where all things come to rest.

Four thriving firemen overflowed our little bathroom
when he couldn't hoist himself from the tub.
He and I, we'd tangled for an hour, tried
everything we could think of,
realized at last we were both too weak.

Firefighters picked him up easy as a cat.
He was wet, leg muscles wasted.
They wrapped him softly in towels.

2. We Learn My Husband Is Ready for a Wheelchair

Three laid-back firemen parked
under the jacarandas, sauntered
past the lemon tree into the garage
to extract him from the car, passenger side.

He'd wedged himself into the well
trying to stand up and grab his walker.
He'd forbidden me to buy a wheelchair.
He didn't want to look old.

They told us to find wheels or else
go to the ER, that summer Saturday night.
How, how to roll him into the house?
Clever firemen, they propped him on a hand truck,
secured him close with bungee cords.
Had they learned to think slant,
or had they seen *Silence of the Lambs*?

My pacifist husband, now turned parcel and patient,
slumped against his binding of bungee cords.
They turned him into Hannibal Lecter minus the muzzle,
transported him inert as a water heater.

3. We Learn Not to Wait

His heart trilled a drumroll
when I laid my ear to his chest. So fast
the blood can't move, and throws clots,
and everything stops.

Six sturdy firemen plus a farm boy of a trainee.
And a gurney plus equipment. And paperwork.
I'd learned to be ready. I handed them
the updated printouts:
the list of meds, the timeline
of diagnosis and surgery, recent treatments.

They jammed the IV into his carotid,
inserted it hasty, any old how,
to stop his heart to restart his heart.
How that flatline on the EKG froze me.
The firemen exuded health
sharp as lemon blossom, promising as plum.

Then the living room, big enough to receive them,
abruptly vacant. Sunlight
laying chambers on the carpet.
Trailing trampled jacaranda blossom,
they'd rushed him out to the ambulance.

GIFTS OF THE WHITE DOG

when the White Dog howls in front of a house where someone is ill
    sniffing out landmines and trapped people
when the White Dog raises his hackles
    refuses to sniff your hand
when the White Dog flattens his ears
    refuses to know your voice
when the White Dog howls at the open door for no reason
    and digs a hole in your garden

when the White Dog sleeps, paws curled, tail outstretched
    after digging a hole in your garden
when the White Dog howls outside at night
when the White Dog howls three times, then falls silent
when the White Dog howls once, then falls silent

perhaps the White Dog empowers and enlivens you, like yeast
perhaps the White Dog asks to become part of your life stream
perhaps the White Dog longs to meet others like you
perhaps these acts do not signal a breakthrough

perhaps the White Dog adores you
perhaps the White Dog believes you
perhaps the White Dog is light and shadow
    in vibrational affinity
perhaps the White Dog consoles you
when the White Dog says   *Maybe it's yours, but it's never personal*

THE SOLDIER'S LAST WORDS, CO-AXIAL

Let us

cross over

the river and

rest

in the shade

of the trees

Suppose you could

land where

the river alone would flow. Sleep

-less. Counting sheep

could work.

Let their sighs drown out the world

crashing down around you.

I HELP MY HUSBAND SLEEP

I smell your silver hair,
Einstein-wild from hospital sweat,
waxy under my hand.
Your head rolls onto my shoulder, crushes
my hair so it rasps in my ear.
Me under you, offering myself
as a better bed, compressing
the single-use egg-crate mattress.
I lie braced in this narrow bed
that keeps me from cradling you enough.
Stop fighting your eyelids' pull.
Burrow your heavy head into my breast.
Take up your dreams,
like a tired dog who feels the grass
under his paws, twitching in his sleep
at the flicker of abundant rabbits.
What am I for, but to let you let down.

COMEBACK

1.

If it comes back we'll get chemo, you said,
not remembering   how, even then,
  no one wanted chemo for a man eighty-seven
  and it was now two years on.
I tried to remind you,
but you took memory for granted, you believed what you recalled.

so no chemo, just whatever made the passage lighter,
  But chemo's the protocol   *that's what they all said*
Sure—the protocol for someone
with a drop more than fumes in the tank
and so, dear heart, not for you.

2.

When it came back you started dying faster.
  You died of not living,
recalling but not remembering,
  and kind drugs helped carry you off

So you talked about chemo, and I sat.
  silent and heavy in my chair,
  seeing the empty room behind you,
knowing the world to come. You were not remembering
we'd already had that conversation with Dr. Patel.

My hand still (remembering) your every dip and curve.

3.

Dr. Patel, so dapper in those custom-fitted shirts
so pleased when we admired
the candy-striped buttons,
the cloth figured with tiny blue flowers,
such noblesse oblige when he praised
the shirt I'd given you for our last anniversary.

Tears stood in his eyes when he told us
    I'd make you comfortable
    You'd feel as little as you wanted
   Little was not what you wanted to feel.
   Nothing was not what you wanted to feel.
   Nothing was never what we wanted.

BLACK HOLE

The Schwarzschild radius slid past last week
My mouth moved   no sound got out
Only the black hole forming at the center
kept our galaxy from flying apart

Why send bulletins
Everyone is receding at light-speed
and nothing can arrive   nothing can escape
For now, you still have your spin
your strangeness
your charm

From where I stand
I can see the future
I smell its disinfectant
There go your molecules being stripped
in the first trillion-trillionth
of that new universe

And the black hole is in your lung
You're still wracked by the slam
of that singular contraction
before the new universe started to expand
You are everything you always were
The future will never arrive

ROCKET SCIENTIST

The techs have strapped you in,
launched you under the scanner.
Already I have to look away.
I veil my eyes with a word game on my phone,
but the next word is **m o r t a l**.

Your pelvic arch on the screen, and the lit fuse
of your unfolding spine,
both sprout little galaxies.
Nebulae shine through old dust,
through dark matter
no matter the point of view.
That blazing node is the lodestone,
pointing to the star in the North,
the hub of our circling concern.

The traveling table takes your grainy feet.
The screen transmutes them
into a low-gravity jump, a deliberated Rapture.
The screen sits high up,
like the cabin screen in coach on Pan Am.
Those old flights seemed endless.

Each sparkling toe freezes me.
Your liver full of half-lives unlived
is a quasar of particle decay, bright galaxies
invaded, half a half-life flaring out.
Quick, look up. A falling star.

WHAT TO SAY TO WELL-MEANING BUT UNTHINKING PEOPLE

Not a roller coaster
more like the Gravitron, the turbine
starting with a lurch,
spinning faster and faster
You are pinned against the walls,
left upright
while the floor drops out
    from under your feet

Not lost in a dark wood
more like driving on a foggy night
All you've got is parking lights
showing only the bit of road
just ahead
Something looms behind you
You are overtaken
before you can even think
    what was that

Not like an old bad dream
where you already know what comes next
Not even the sick certainty
that flying means falling soon
the only sure thing being
    you cannot wake up,
    being already awake

Not a whole new world
more like an old place you've never been to
though you recognize
the landmarks
    the used car lots
    the Stardust motel
    the Shalimar bar
    the no-kill shelter on Bon View
generic and inevitable
as the fabric art
in the corridors
    of the hospital

an apple before the first bite

EVERGREENS

You're old enough to flinch
when they mangle *Alzheimer's* to *old-timer's*.
People give advice
about people like you, urge
trying out chair yoga, making new friends.
You can garden in boxes,
set up an herb garden,
parsley or sage, rosemary and thyme.

You remember hiking the pass
over Baldy, the John Muir Trail,
attaining the other side of the mountain.
Your wife cultivates a smaller patch, applying
gray water, red vitamins, mounds of mulch
to slow down the using up, the parching out.
You watch the finches splashing the birdbath dry.

Trade the finches now
for woodpeckers feasting
on new grubs in dead wood. Trade
green shade for silvery leaves,
for two-day cactus flowers
revealing their short-lived pure silk petals.
You see the true nature of *xeriscape*
unmasked as *zeroscape*. Evergreen oldies twist
in your head. *Are you going to Scarborough Fair?*

Already you have traded walking for your walker.
Springy green grass surges treacherous
under your suddenly tentative feet,
prickly, crunching. You miss new green,
new as apertures in the air, new-minted light.
You've traded limber branches
and spendthrift sprays of buds
for lab results, for call buttons. For sticks.

PROPRIOCEPTION

I spread my hand on his chest, feel him only on the pads of my fingertips. Only with the skin, through the dead layer of skin. I feel him by warmth and pressure, proprioception. Where I do not touch him I do not feel. I press harder but the membrane is a thin film, and I feel the membrane more than I feel him. Why should I get up to write this? Why do anything but nestle my cheek into his clean T-shirt, inhale its small breath of open air, even if the rest of me lies without feeling, far away on top of the blankets. Nothing passes through. From this sealed place I know all at once the hole he will leave.

PINES IN THE WIND

Not a duet. More
like call-and-response
popping into punctuating bubbles
breaking the surface
as in a pot of black beans.

He is past words.
I'm hearing new sounds, voices,
each crowding out the last.
That same call-and-response,
another thoughtful guttural
now answered by wind in pines.
Wind swelling, strained through dry branches,
keening through sap-needled pines.

That pine-combed wind
becomes a dog whining,
then shifts back into wind.
Faraway cats crying
on the other side of a door.
A duck, slogging through swampland,
each effort pulling the webs
with a suck, a squelch,
from deep sour mud.

Coughs breaking him.
Outcry just short of shouts
in an aria of protest.
A fit of coughing,
fit to jerk his diaphragm
almost to a retch, fit
to turn his lungs inside-out,
to let us pluck out
tumors, clean as mushrooms,
pluck them out at the last.

AND THEN

How empty his body became
once he'd left it,
his jaw hanging slack, then slacker,
his face emptying, dissolving
into mere parts. Empty of him,
no longer his face. Still his hands.

I still expected him
to pull away
from my tugging fingers
when I tied up a bundle of his silver hair
with a length of thread,
binding a sheaf
before I cut it off.

PIETÀ

Christ has aged on the Cross.
See his ribs, thin, flat, blunt
as a chicken's.
Already His body is heading for skeleton,
knees thicker than his thighs,
feet swollen from the overworked heart,
giving out from all that giving out.

The wasted muscles of your legs,
slight and thin, more taken than given.
Only your swollen feet
showed how your heart
could no longer raise you up.
Mary cradles her Son, having arranged
her stone mantle on stone bench,
and He molds to her, emptied out.

As your heart failed at last
I gripped your hand, tried to tell you
you weren't alone.
When your neck was freed
of resisting, your head rolled loose,
freed of laboring
against the weight of the earth.

We cut away the bile-soaked shirt,
we caressed you anyway with warm sponges
before you grew stone-cold,
we worked you into your favorite shirt
with the tiny blue flowers,
the shirt you and I loved the best.

We washed your vacant body
though I'd already cleansed you
when your bile first rose
at the food you could no longer use
from our shared world.

THE BALLAD OF THE CLAIRVOYANT WIDOW

> —a cento of lines of Christine Gosnay, Michelle
> Brittan Rosado, Russell Salomon, and Theodore
> Roethke

Slow, slow as a fish she came,
A green angel swaying branches.
The wide streams go their way.
Everything undoes itself.
He woke with mountains in his knees.
She saw her father shrinking in his skin.

She thought a bird and it began to fly.
The wings have fallen off. The arms too.
It was as if she tried to walk in hay.
Once she knew how to run.
She came to the western river,
breathed as if moving a hand toward a candle.

The sleep was not deep but waking was slow.
The light cried out, and she was there to hear.
She went in slowly, and found him.
She watched the river wind itself away.
The outline of one is inseparable.
The outline of one is inseparable.

EUREKA

Damn,
that woman showcasing on NPR can sing,
and she misses her man's love.
Belting Burt Bacharach's jaunty grief,
she says her little prayer.

Her son calls her *a warrior butterfly*.
He knows: so much, so much she suffered.
Sometimes she suffered in the garden.
Sometimes at the piano, sometimes in bed.

But her late husband always communicated with her,
　　by voicemail
　　by the slant of the sun
　　by receipts falling out of books.
She was never alone.
Just let me know you're all right,
she implored she required,
and hot damn he let her know. So handy.

So I try it out, why not?
Could you? just to let me know you're all right?
And sure enough, at that precise instant,
I stumble over the cats' canned food,
Chicken and Spinach for Gravy Lovers.
My fleece slipper sops it up,
scatters chunks all over the rag rug
we bought in a fragrant funky store in Eureka
on our honeymoon.

HE NEVER LET ME READ HIS PALM

They'd massaged his face into peace,
the stamp on his passport.
He looked reconciled at last.
He'd never accepted death before,
fought for his next breath
the pauses longer, breaking the thread.
His death-bed face had shown how
empty he was, how worn out.

This restful face looked final, noble,
a much nicer mask for memory.
I came up as a flower child, believing
and not believing fortunes and signs.
He'd never let me read his palm.
Now I could have read his lifeline at last
to see if Death had got it right.
Now there seemed no point.
Always the scientist, boy genius,
he'd no use for fortunetelling.

The mortuary had laid him out in state
for me to see him one last time.
Only his face exposed, hair combed,
wasted body hidden
by the graceful green drape.
No casket. Just a bier, a platform,
a pause before cremation.

CLAWS

—with apologies to Matthew Dickman

MD's grief is a big heavy animal,
a purple gorilla, clearly
more sophisticated than my grief.
Mine is a bear, dull, ponderous, coarsely furred.
An Other, not human, a dark mass,
paws like slices of log.
No thumbs.

My bear lumbers,
sighs like an accordion,
takes up a lot of space in the house.
For months he was always in my room.
I had to edge around him to get out of bed,
to move the cats and feed them.
Someone cleaned the litter boxes.
Must have been me,
though I don't remember.

My bear doesn't speak, doesn't cuddle.
He cannot figure out the TV remote.
Would drugs help?
I don't know the protocols
for lulling a bear.
How much is too much?
and how can you tell?
When do bears move on?

When there's no water to buoy them up,
when their season has run.

Bears do like a hot tub.
I give mine a lot of long baths.
Oh my god, the state of the tub.
And the smell of wet bear.
Like mold, you can never scrub it away.
And I've started thinking about a Roomba.
I just cannot deal with the drifts of shed fur.

I consider the power
of the swipe of the paw.
And those claws.
No one wants to talk about claws
wielded by an irritable bear.
The heavy bluntness.
I consider the actions
leading to a necklace.
What should a bear claw necklace mean?

ALBUM: PORTRAIT WITH PANAMA HAT

Ganders at the field's edge guarded the goslings and fledglings,
    honked once when we approached. See, they've all turned
    and fled.

Here we are standing deep inside the hawthorn bushes.
    Proust had allergies, dared view flowers only through the
    window.

Our friend made a special detour to this village,
    all streets paved with unself-conscious cobblestones.

That's the village bakery renowned for the true macarons,
    the best macarons, the ones worth the excursion.

She took us to this auberge whose resident dog
    favored you with chin on thigh, true love
    from liquid brown eyes.

I remember air heavy with humid heat. The photo shows only
    the warmth I found against your shoulder.

After that luncheon, we ambled through the town.
    Here's the local Gothic cathedral where we ended up.

That parabola of bullet holes in the limestone wall must have been
    from *métrailleurs,* Resistance machine guns
    driving out Nazis.

Here. Let me show you.

WHAT REMAINS

I left your heart up in Montmartre,
I missed your lips in Montparnasse.
Stood at the bench where you, ecstatic,
sat to marvel at the leaves.

I threw your ashes in the Seine,
concealed by night, so no one saw.
But you would know where they had fallen,
sunk, downstream from Notre-Dame.

When Notre-Dame went up in flames
I thought of bringing ashes there,
where dried remains of martyred saints
were soon to billow from the fire.

We'd hung a lock on Pont des Arts,
let fall the key. Then we embraced.
I never thought to see your bones
go sifting down into the murk.

You never knew how much I feared
the cancer that attacked your bones.
I'd known for months, back from the time
I'd sat and watched the PET scan run.

Those gritty plaques, were they your spine,
the relics that the cancer left?
those green-gray ashes, more like sand
than fire's soot, than shell of flesh.

OLD WOOD

(On April 15 2019, Notre-Dame de Paris was half-destroyed by an electrical fire)

Halfway through my last dinner,
my phone showed me the blaze,
unfathomable, inconceivable
as the Grand Canyon creaking shut.

Incredulous, the bistro owner confirmed:
Everyone on staff is watching.
You'll need a chocolate dessert.

And firefighters poured the river onto the flames.
The spire lifted as it came loose, and people gasped.
They wailed as though a suicide had jumped.

The spring day before, I'd walked the quais,
browsed the stalls of the bouquinistes,
shot mood pics of the squared-off towers,
total cornball, through the mist of new leaves.

Arrow of God. The spire fell
before the sun was down,
The fire turned the sky red,
burned the cross white-hot.

Not all the water in the world could help,
not even the fire boats, water cannons pumping the river.
Parisians stood and watched, sang and wept.

We all hoped for rain. Rain came the next morning.

Ash sifted down. catching, reflecting coral light
I'd brought my husband's ashes in a carved wooden box.
No need, no need. Plenty of ash to go around.

After dinner, the owner walked me to the door.
We sniffed the air,
caught the wildfire smell
everyone from SoCal already knows.
Vieux bois, she shrugged, wincing. Old wood.

ROBOCALL/ REMAINS

—message found on voicemail

Hello, I'm Pastor Hank

Caring for you, my love,
I just escaped

from the Very Good Bible Church

Hell, whose memories
were a noose that

Truth and Liberty Schools

never loosened.
How to believe

We have a blessing for you

in cool air, soft light, when
each breath is dying and

You can realize: God loves you

seeing the dying
over and again

to recognize him as your Savior

rips and overturns
my heart

Lord forgive me, Lord save me

again. I am no Dante,
cannot live only to be

Leave your number

made up of days given
to remembering

we'll call you back

as though anything ever
could rouse you from
your jar of ashes.

SNAKE RIVER

Back when it was a treat
    to sleep in tents on the ground,
we rafted down the Snake River,
    in Wyoming or Montana.

Loaded with us eight tourists,
    the raft floated low in the water,
sunrise too recent to send
    more than a glint off the ripples.

We caught the smell off the banks,
    fresh and rank,
horsetail and coral cannas
    growing and rotting,
loose bits feeding fish that drew
    the adolescent eagle
jumping from a sandbar flat-taloned
    into the water,
refusing to swoop and scoop.

Such a stubborn teenager of a bird.
All the fish could see him coming.

A young moose's antlers parted the cattails,
    brown-gray nose like a wet sock
announcing the preposterous head
    before the knobby knees emerged.

That morning I sat with you at my back.
    You shielded me from the other tourists
tittering and sneering how they hated California.
    I shielded you from the pull of the raft edge,
pulling you as edges always did,
    always fearsome, full of peril.

The air floating off the water, soft on my face.
    One hand holding yours,
the other trailing fingers through the river.
    Luscious passage of the ripples
    telling my fingers
    the ride was nearly over.

BEAUTIFUL LEAVES

It turned out *pot-au-feu* was plain boiled beef.
You ate only the luscious marrow, mashed
on a chunk of baguette.
The wine was house red soft as moss.
We'd ordered only a quarter liter, but
the host timed his pours, at least four.
When you laughed,
he passed the neck of the bottle unseen
under your evoking hand.
I caught the host's eye
    what are you doing
he shot me a smile
    I am making him happy.

Chairs rested upended on tables.
We were last to leave.
I helped you with your raincoat.
You raised your face to the city stars,
tipped back hard onto the window box,
flattened the geraniums.
I hoisted you past the music store
    on rue Léopold Robert,
past the neon reflections
    of the boul' Raspail.

On the corner of Edgar Quinet
you sank onto the friendly bench
under the streetlamp's yellow sphere
filtered by new chestnut leaves.
Look at the leaves
the beautiful leaves
I've never seen
such beautiful leaves.

So I sat down beside you, I looked
at those illuminated leaves,
outlined in absinthe and lamplight.
I was tired, wanted back to our flat.
I didn't know what you knew:
the host had poured happiness,
the leaves were mystic love,
time was up for the last time,
you'd never see new leaves again.

You, exalted, clear-minded, unswerving,
you knew the night should never end.

ACKNOWLEDGMENTS

I wish to thank the editors of the following publications where some of these poems first appeared in similar form.

Algebra of Owls: I Help My Husband Sleep
Atticus Review: Rocket Scientist
CHEST, Pectoriloquy: Black Hole; What I Reply to Well-Meaning People; Proprioception
Forage: Beautiful Leaves
Gyroscope Review: Claws; Eureka
MacQueen's Quinterly: Evergreens
New Verse News: Old Wood
Otoliths: The Soldier's Last Words, co-axial
Redheaded Stepchild: The Beautiful Story
Right Hand Pointing: And then
Sad Girls Blog: Snake River
Spillway: Pietà
Unlost: Ballad of the Clairvoyant Widow (a cento); Gifts of the White Dog

ABOUT THE AUTHOR

Karen Greenbaum-Maya worked as a clinical psychologist for 35 years. She earned her B.A. from Reed College in 1973 and her Ph.D. from the California School of Professional Psychology in 1982. She has managed a congressional campaign, has sung in a local opera company, and has developed cookie recipes for commercial use. She reviewed restaurants for the *Claremont Courier* for five years, sometimes in heroic couplets, sometimes imitating Hemingway. She shared her life with her late husband for 34 years, which were not enough.

She returned to poetry in 2008. Since then, her poems received Special Merit and Honorable Mention in the Muriel Craft Bailey Memorial contest from Marge Piercy and from B.F. Fairchild. Other poems have appeared in *B O D Y, Sow's Ear Poetry Review, Comstock Poetry Review, Heron Tree, Waccamaw, Spillway, Measure,* and *Rappahannock Poetry Review.* She co-curates Fourth Saturdays, a monthly poetry series in Claremont, California, and Garden of Verses, an annual day-long reading of nature poems in Claremont's California Botanic Garden. Kattywompus Press publishes her three chapbooks, *Burrowing Song* (2013), *Eggs Satori* (2014), and, *Kafka's Cat* (2019). Kelsay Books publishes her full-length collection *The Book of Knots and their Untying* (2016).

112 N. Harvard Ave. #65
Claremont, CA 91711

chapbooks@bamboodartpress.com

www.bamboodartpress.com

CPSIA information can be obtained
at www.ICGtesting.com
Printed in the USA
JSHW052146260723
45455JS00002B/60

9 781947 240872